FREEDOM
Human Codes No Machine Can Crack
By Mehta

Teach. What Can't Be Googled.
Create. What Can't Be Copied.
Live. What Can't Be Faked.

This book won't give you the answers.
It will awaken the creator in you who already has them.

Copyright © 2025 – MEHTAARTS

All rights to this book are reserved.

No permission is given for any part of this book to be reproduced,
transmitted in any form or means; electronic or mechanical,
stored in a retrieval system, photocopied, recorded, scanned, or otherwise.
Personal annotations within this book are intended for individual use only
and may not be reproduced, shared, or distributed in any form without
prior written consent from the author.

Digital reproduction, including screenshots, uploads,
or sharing of any content (including annotated pages) via online platforms,
is strictly prohibited without written permission.

Any of these actions require the proper written permission of Mehta the author.
Unauthorised use may result in legal action. For permission requests or inquiries,
contact the author at MEHTAARTS.COM.

FREEDOM

Human Codes No Machine Can Crack

By Mehta

Teach. What Can't Be Googled.
Create. What Can't Be Copied.
Live. What Can't Be Faked.

Available from Amazon, Apple Books, Barnes & Noble, Walmart and other retail outlets.

ISBN: 978-1-9192379-1-6 (Hardcover)
ISBN: 978-1-9192379-0-9 (Paperback)
ISBN: 978-1-9192379-2-3 (eBook)
First Printing Edition, 2025

Don't Just Read This Book. Use It.

This book grows as you do.
Open it anywhere.
Every page is a spark.
Some chapters leave you with Takeaways you can carry straight into your work.
Others offer a Wonder, a question to open you wider.
A few give you a Practice, something to test in the real world.
Not every page gives you all three. That's the point.

The rhythm shifts so you don't just read at one pace.
You live it at your own pace.

Keep it close. Write in it. Scream at it. Hug it.
Put a page where you will see it.
Come back when you are stuck.
Come back when you're unstoppable.
Come back when you feel nothing at all.
Enjoy the book. Celebrate what's already yours.

About The Author.

Mehta is a globally acclaimed, award-winning creative leader and artist who works with future-focused companies around the world, blending creativity, care, and technology to help brands build emotional connection and drive growth that lasts.

Collectors of Mehta's artwork include a Silicon Valley icon, a spiritual leader, a music mogul, a multi-billionaire, and global CEOs. His pieces live in homes, studios, and offices around the world, and feature in the Mehta Private Exhibition held in New York, London, and Mumbai.

The book's methods didn't arrive as wisdom for Mehta.
They began as questions about creating when nothing felt original, leading when he didn't belong, and holding identity while the rules kept shifting.

Those questions became codes for how to create, lead, and change through every part of life.

They're not just his anymore.

They're a lens. A rhythm. A field guide for those who feel the world shifting under their feet, and want to shape what comes next.

Industry Icons Mehta Has Worked With.

These are leaders and change-makers I've had the privilege to collaborate with. What mattered most wasn't their titles, but the work, the late nights, the questions, and the shared search for truth. Their standards pushed me, their trust grounded me, and their vision shaped the possibilities we built together.

"Mehta has great energy and is solution oriented."
ALLISON JOHNSON
CO-FOUNDER, THE INSTITUTE FOR MORAL IMAGINATION

"Mehta moves with soul, vision, and purpose. He doesn't just create he shifts culture."
KEVIN LILES
FORMER PRESIDENT OF DEF JAM, CEO OF 300 ENTERTAINMENT

"Mehta is a key member of the launch of Reliance Jio. I am very proud of his achievements."
MUKESH AMBANI
FOUNDER & CHAIRMAN, RELIANCE JIO

"Collaboration, innovation and storytelling is what you get working with Mehta."
PRATIK THAKAR
GLOBAL VP OF GENERATIVE AI, THE COCA-COLA COMPANY

"I appreciate Mehta's contribution and passion for S4. We want to build something that challenges the industry."
SIR MARTIN SORRELL
FOUNDER WPP & CHAIRMAN, S4 CAPITAL GROUP

This Is Not A Book. It Is A System Upgrade.

If your soul had a software update, it wouldn't fix the bugs.
It would delete half the apps, give you your mornings back,
and make you remember why you're here.
Freedom works the same way.
You don't notice you've lost it until you're on autopilot, swiping,
scrolling, performing your way through the day.

You don't need another productivity hack
or a life coach yelling at you to crush it.
You need a whole new operating system
that puts your humanity back in charge,
so human, it's dangerous.
If you've ever felt like you're drowning in noise,
scrolling more than creating,
or leading without feeling, this book is for you.
It's written for creatives, leaders, fearless founders,
and the artist in the boardroom, for anyone who knows
the most powerful work is born where spirit and strategy meet.

You've felt it.
Everything looks right,
but something in you says, "This is not it."
That's your signal to go deeper.

Mindset. Habits. Hustle.
They got you this far.
They won't take you where you're going.
This is your upload.
Your Freedom codes.
To living, creating, and leading from what cannot be copied,
from the part of you no machine can touch.

New Intelligence. Fresh Approach.

Super-intelligent machines will out-think and out-create us.
It will solve problems before we name them,
extend us in extraordinary ways, but it will never be us.
It can't miss someone.
It can't hear a song and know why it matters.
It can't turn pain into beauty or speak truth with a trembling voice.

Feeling is your edge.
It's the rarest and most needed intelligence of the future.

That's where this book begins,
with the operating system only you can run.
It's not a checklist.
It's a rhythm.
Three codes to carry into everything you make
and everything you are.

Teach. What can't be Googled.
Create. What can't be copied.
Live. What can't be faked.

These aren't ideas to study.
They're lived.
The deeper you live them, the more they live in you.

TEACH

Wisdom over information.

Signals only you can send, the kind that stay with people long after the meeting, the dinner, or the chance encounter.

CREATE

Soul over output.

Work that carries your fingerprint.

The piece only you could make, in the way only you could make it.

LIVE

Presence over performance.

A life full from the inside out.

The kind that makes the room shift the second you walk in.

The future will never ask you to keep up.

It will ask you to stand out.

To show up so fully human that even the machines take notes.

Let's begin.

Are You Creating Or Just Copying?
Stop chasing trends. Make what only you can make.

Is The Life You're Building Even Yours?
Strip out the noise. Build from what feels true.

What If Business Had A Soul Again?
Lead with presence. Create work that outlives the campaign.

What If Your Intuition Was The Strategy?
Trust your signal. Move before the brief arrives.

Are You Living Fully Or Just Performing Well?
Trade applause for alignment. Live the life that matches your truth.

The Grain Of Rice. 2

Don't Wait To Be Chosen. 7

The Personal Blueprint. 12

Places Are Soul Signatures. 18

Pain As Portal. 24

Talk To The Brand Like It's Alive. 32

Make New Mistakes. 42

Redesign The Room. 49

Shape What Only You Can. 56

Break The Frame. 62

Art As A Spiritual Weapon. 69

Own Happy. 74

There Are No Answers. 80

The Creative Spirit. 87

Love Over Everything. 92

The Operating System In Motion. 99

Live Transmission. 105

Part I. TEACH.
Teach What Can't Be Googled.

We live in a world drowning in instant answers. But wisdom was never meant to be copy-pasted. This part is about rediscovering the questions only you can ask, the ones that no machine can answer, the ones that make you human.

Chapter 1
The Grain Of Rice.

Why Destiny Isn't A Plan.
TEACH: What Can't Be Googled.

When I was nine, my mother made a pot of rice.
Nothing special, no spices. Just water, heat, and time.

Then, friends arrived unexpectedly.
They sat, ate, laughed, and left.

She turned to me and said:
"Look? I made rice.
Some came. Some ate. Some didn't.
If your name is on a grain of rice, it is meant for you.
You own it.
If it's not, it never was. That's destiny, my son."
I never forgot it, not as a lesson, but as a code.

Destiny is never about effort or luck.
It's about tuning into a signal that's already looking for you.
A frequency, not a formula.
Think of frequency as the state of creative flow,
that rare moment when ideas align, timing clicks,
and you feel perfectly in sync with yourself or your work.
You may have felt this before.
When instinct outshone any plan.
When you just knew without proof.
You don't chase it. You feel it,
the way you sense someone you love is about to call.
The more you tune in, the clearer it becomes.

Like the rice in my mother's pot,
your mind has been quietly preparing

for moments like this all your life.
It notices what you miss, stores what you forget,
and keeps it simmering in the background.
Then, without warning, it serves you the answer, no proof,
no plan, just a knowing.

That's instinct. A lifetime of patterns, disguised as a single grain of clarity. The mind is always working ahead of you.
It gathers moments, sights, sounds, glances, fragments of memory, and threads them together until they form something solid enough to trust. By the time you "just know," your inner world has already been making sense of the outer one.

It's not magic.
It's memory, emotion,
and experience quietly agreeing on the same truth.
Being in alignment doesn't mean everything will fall into place.
Sometimes you'll be out of sync for years,
and that's still part of the path.
The work is yours. The outcome isn't.
You can plan it all perfectly despite that,
some bowls of rice will stay untouched.

That's not a failure. That's the flow.

Since that day, I've worked with billionaires, brands, and movements.
I've sat in rooms of power and possibility.
But it always comes back to that kitchen, that bowl of rice,
that silence, that instinct.

Takeaways

Destiny is alignment, not control. Alignment only happens when you keep tuning in and showing up, ready for when the spark arrives.

Being in alignment doesn't mean everything falls into place, sometimes you'll be out of sync for years, and that's still part of the path.

Instinct is your mind's way of revealing the work, it's already done for you.

Your space to capture the ideas that won't let you go. Write it. Sketch it. Keep it.

Chapter 2
Don't Wait To Be Chosen.

Self Selection Is Power.
TEACH: What Can't Be Googled.

For years, I waited.

Waited for the right client.
Waited for the right mentor.
Waited to be noticed.
To be tapped.
To be told, "You're the one."
I believed that if I worked hard enough, stayed humble, and played the part, someone would eventually point to me and say, Now. You've earned it.

But the call never came.

No one tells you this.
I wasn't told this, I had to find it out the hard way.

No one is coming to pick you.

Not from the mountaintop.
Not from the algorithm.
Not from the boardroom with the big names.
No one is coming to pick you.
Stop waiting for the tap on the shoulder.

The real shift happened the moment I stopped waiting.
The moment I decided.
I don't need to be chosen.
I choose myself.

There were no announcements, no strategy presentation,
no "10 steps to becoming undeniable."
Just a quiet, radical choice.
To build before being validated.
To speak before being invited.
To create before being funded.
To lead before being approved.

That's when everything started moving.
Not because I knew what I was doing,
but because I finally knew who I was.
Move as if it's already yours.
Energy and courage create momentum long before recognition does.

We respond to action faster than we do to opportunity.
The moment you take a step, your mind rewrites the story,
shifting from maybe to already.
That quiet inner voice begins to believe you're in motion,
and belief has a way of pulling reality toward it.
Some of my biggest breakthroughs didn't come from getting the role.
They came from showing up like I already had it.

With energy.
With soul.
With nothing to prove and everything to give.
Not everyone can walk into a boardroom or launch a company overnight. That's not the point. Choosing yourself is not about scale, more about signaling.

It can start as small as raising your hand in a meeting, posting an idea online, gathering a few people around a kitchen table.
Every act of self-selection carries the same energy.
What matters is that you stop waiting for someone else to anoint you, and begin practicing the truth that you're already enough to begin.
Too many of us are still performing.
We're missing the ones bold enough to stop asking for permission.
The artists.
The founders.
The storytellers.
The spiritual builders.

They don't wait.
They pick themselves.
They build the room.
They show the world what it didn't know was missing.
Power isn't given. It's remembered.
You already carry what you've been waiting for.

Takeaways

Power begins the moment you decide to move,
not when someone says you can.

Action rewires belief, and belief reshapes reality.

Self-selection is the first act of true leadership.

Your space to capture the ideas that won't let you go. Write it. Sketch it. Keep it.

Chapter 3
The Personal Blueprint.

Your Inner Architecture.
TEACH: What Can't Be Googled.

Some truths don't arrive as words.
They arrive as a sudden heat in your chest.
A flicker in the fog.
A moment you can't explain, only follow.

That's your blueprint, not a plan.
Not a strategy.
A code you've been carrying since the beginning.

You don't have to invent it.
You only have to remember it.

Destiny is not a finish line you run toward.
It's a vibration you already sense, even if you've been ignoring it.

It's why some ideas won't leave you alone.
Why certain rooms feel alive the moment you step in.

You don't follow it with certainty.
You follow it with trust.
The compass is already in you.

Rebellion is not chaos.
It's the quiet decision to stop folding yourself
into shapes that don't fit.
It's the refusal to keep living by rules you never agreed to.
It's not about breaking for the sake of breaking,
it's about building from somewhere true.

Take the fashion designer and icon Coco Chanel. She didn't just
design clothes. She rewrote what women could wear,
and who they were allowed to be.

When corsets and constraints defined femininity,
she trusted a different compass.
Coco Chanel cut away the excess.
She chose freedom over formality.
She borrowed from menswear,
freaked out the establishment, and ignored the rules.

It wasn't strategy.
It wasn't trend.
It was a blueprint.

A refusal to fold herself into shapes that didn't fit.

What she created wasn't just fashion. It was liberation.
Women could move. Work. Breathe differently.
Chanel refused to wait for permission.
She built from what felt true in her bones.

Melanie Perkins built Canva after 100+ investor rejections,
proof that playful, simple design can scale into a $25 billion platform.

That's the power of inner architecture.
Design not as decoration, but as rebellion.

Here's the thing, before you can even explain it,
your mind automatically notices patterns.
It gathers moments, experiences, and emotions into
a kind of inner map.
Your personal architecture.
When you act in alignment with it, things feel easier,
lighter, almost inevitable.
When you move against it, everything feels heavier than it should.

Story is the thread that pulls it all together.
It's not a sales pitch.
It's how we stay human.
How we carry meaning across miles and generations.
How pain becomes purpose.
How confusion finds its shape.

The right story doesn't just move others.
It brings you back to yourself.
Destiny gives you direction.
Rebellion gives you courage.
Story gives you meaning.

This is your blueprint.
No one else can write it.
It's not here to be memorised.
It's here to be lived.

Takeaways

Your blueprint is already within you, it's remembered, not invented.

The mind collects your lived patterns into a map you can trust.

Destiny, rebellion, and story are the three pillars
of your inner architecture.

Wonder

Where is your compass already pointing?
What rule no longer fits you?
What story are you here to tell?

Practice - Activate Your Blueprint

Write three words.
One for your Destiny. What's pulling you forward?
One for your Rebellion. What you refuse to repeat.
One for your Story. What you want to matter.
Pick one.
Ask. What would it look like to live this today?
Take one small step towards it, then notice what changes.

Your space to capture the ideas that won't let you go. Write it. Sketch it. Keep it.

Chapter 4
Places Are Soul Signatures.

The Geography Of Growth.
TEACH: What Can't Be Googled.

Every place leaves a mark.
Not just in your memory,
but in your cadence.
In the way you think.
In the way you move through the world.

Some places quicken your heartbeat,
telling you to pay attention.
Others slow your breath.
Some sharpen you.
Others soften you.
If you're paying attention,
you realise places don't just hold your story,
they help write it.

London gave me discipline and defiance.
New York gave me appetite and urgency.
Mumbai gave me speed and soul.
Singapore gave me structure and stillness.
San Francisco gave me ideas.
Los Angeles gave me light.
Wales gave me depth.

These weren't just places.
They were portals.

Each one sharpened my instinct,
tuning me toward what mattered.
Each one became part of my voice.

A place is never just a backdrop.
It's a co-author.

The air, the streets, the light, the pace, the people.
They shape what you create and how you create it.

The mind adapts to its environment faster than we realise.
Walk into a city that hums with urgency,
and your thoughts race to match it.
Step into stillness, and your inner noise begins to settle.
Your surroundings don't just influence how you feel in the moment,
they train the tempo of your thinking,
and that tempo shapes the work you make.

No need for you to cross continents to feel this.
A girl sketching in the back of a cafe in Tokyo,
tuning out the chaos to find her own stillness.
A guy skateboarding through the same street in Spain every day,
learning the flow of his city and his own momentum.
Everywhere hums with its own resonance if you listen closely.

Some places awaken your ambition.
Some give you silence to hear yourself again.
Some teach you to be seen.
Some teach you to disappear and return different.

If you feel stuck,
it might not be your ideas,
it might be your environment.

Sometimes you don't need a new plan.
You just need new air.

Takeaways

Places are not passive, they are active co-authors in your story.

Your surroundings set the rhythm of your mind and your creativity.

Sometimes growth comes not from pushing harder, but from changing your environment.

Wonder

Where in the world do you feel most awake?
What local place unlocked something you didn't know was in you?
What city or town isn't just where you are,
but part of who you've become?

Practice - Trace Your Geography of Growth

Where you've been has shaped who you are. Now let it speak.
List three places that left a mark on your rhythm,
a city, a street, a house, even a room.
Next to each, write the one thing it taught you
(e.g. "London was defiance," "Singapore was stillness").
Choose the one that still lives in your bones.
Ask yourself. What part of me came alive there.
What did I remember?
Let that memory guide you today,
in a choice, a sentence, or a way of showing up.

Sometimes the place isn't calling you back.
It's calling something forward.

Your space to capture the ideas that won't let you go. Write it. Sketch it. Keep it.

Chapter 5
Pain As Portal.

Let It Break You Open.
TEACH: What Can't Be Googled.

Pain strips the performance off you.
Not the pain you post about, the real kind.
The private kind.

The call that never came.
The partner who took your work and passed it off as their own.
The person who said forever and meant something shorter.

That kind of pain rearranges your operating system in the dark.
I've known it.

Each moment hurt.
Each one forced a choice.
Shrink or evolve.
Harden or open.

Not all pain is a teacher.
Some pain just takes.
Some seasons are just survival.
Pain doesn't ruin you.
It reveals you.
It breaks the shell around your voice.
It interrupts the performance.
It confronts you with what still needs to be felt.

If you let it, pain doesn't just ache.
It transforms.

But transformation doesn't come from the pain itself.
It comes from the people, places, and practices that help you carry it until you can see what's on the other side.

The mind is built to protect you from pain, to numb you.
Distract you, or turn you away.
But when you stay with it instead of running, something shifts.
Your inner story reshapes, turning wounds into doorways.
The wound stops being the whole truth and becomes the doorway to a deeper one.

Most people try to outrun it.
To brand their way out of heartbreak.
To hustle past the ache.
To design a life where nothing gets too close again.
But the ones who grow, the ones who change the room when they walk in, they don't dodge pain.
They walk through it.
Barefoot.
Eyes wide open.

Some of the most resonant art, music, movements,
and inventions were built through wounds.
Not from the surface.
From the scar.

And sometimes, even in the ache,
you catch yourself laughing at something small,
like a dog chasing its own tail (why do dogs do that?),
proof the light still knows how to find you.

It's the founder who shows up to the pitch
the morning after their biggest loss,
still leading, even with the wound unhealed.
It's the artist who turns heartbreak into a song that fills a stadium.
It's the maker who carries their scar into the work and lets it
change what they create.

The ache became an instruction.
The wound became a doorway.

I can still remember leaving a meeting
where my ideas were dismissed before they were heard.
It felt like a deep failure.
But it was the start of learning to see through other people's eyes,
their hopes, their fears, their reasons why.
So, if you're in pain now, don't rush.
Don't repackage it as wisdom before it's ready.
Stay with it long enough to hear what it's asking of you.
Name it.
Learn from it.
When you're ready, create with it.
Let the pain say what the performance couldn't.
It's never easy to do, but it's worth it.

Takeaways

Pain isn't weakness. It's an invitation.

The wound is not the end. It's a doorway.

What breaks you can also break you open.

Wonder

What wound shaped you more than any applause ever did?
Where have you mistaken survival for healing?
What if the version of you that's crumbling is only a mask?

Practice - Write From The Wound

Not everything broken needs fixing.
Some things need naming.
Recall one moment that changed you, not because it was fair or easy,
but because it cracked something open.

Write a letter to that moment.
Not to resolve it.
Just to acknowledge it.
Say what you couldn't say then.

Read it back slowly.
Notice what rises, a truth, a sentence, a silence.

That's not weakness.
That's your new strength forming.
The pain didn't close you.
It cleared the way.

Your space to capture the ideas that won't let you go. Write it. Sketch it. Keep it.

Part II. CREATE.

Create What Can't Be Copied.

Machines can mimic almost anything, except the beautiful chaos of emotions and mistakes. Originality doesn't come from control. It comes from the risks you take, the flaws you don't edit out, the truth only you can leave behind.

Chapter 6
Talk To The Brand Like It's Alive.

Soul Over Slogan.
CREATE: What Can't Be Copied.

Every brand wants to be loved.
Most end up just yelling.

If you stopped talking, would anyone lean in?

They show up dressed perfectly.
Slogan tight. Values polished. Logo sharp.
They flood your feed. Fill rooms with decks and data.

They chase attention as if it's affection.
A slogan is what you sell. A soul is what they buy.
Underneath it all?
Fear.
Fear of being ignored.
Fear of being misunderstood.
Fear of being forgettable.

And if fear is running the brand, who's really in charge?

I've sat in rooms with some of the world's biggest companies.
The best of them are brilliantly run, alive with curiosity and truth.
Others are still learning to trust that same spirit, and that's where the real breakthroughs wait.
The brief says, "Innovate."
What they really mean is, "Make us feel safe."
They ask for a story.
What they want is a slogan.
They say "connection" but speak like machines.

That's the real gap.
Not a creative one.
A spiritual one.

Then there was Apple.
I've been lucky to work with some of the team.
Apple is built on layers of brilliant strategy, design, tech,
products, and marketing.
But within a project I worked on, four words guided everything.

Make It Feel Human.
That principle cut deep.
No funnel. No framework. No fear.

When's the last time you made something human first,
and strategic second?

Not perfect.
Not polished.
Human.
They weren't chasing trends.
They were chasing truth.
Not metrics. Meaning.
We didn't start with a traditional strategy.
We started with silence.

Then we asked.
What are we afraid to say?
What would this whisper to someone in love?
What do we believe, even if it never sells?

In that pause, the noise dropped.
The surface cracked.
Something real got in.

Not a campaign. A connection.
Not a product. A signal.
Brands aren't machines.
They're mirrors.
They reflect the people who built them.
Their longing, their contradictions, their truth.

Some never listen.
Perfect branding. Perfect product. Perfect campaign.
On paper.

But their questions are about competitors, not customers.
About how to look different, not how to feel true.

The launch campaign spikes.
Clicks come. Likes come.
Six months later, silence.

If a brand can't speak honestly to itself,
it won't speak honestly to anyone.

Nike isn't a shoe. It's the victory. The athlete.
The voice in your head that says, "Go anyway."

Coca-Cola isn't sugar water.
It's togetherness. A moment. A promise shared and chased.

Apple isn't a device.
It's an invitation to create differently, with beauty,
with soul, with care.

Jio isn't just data.
It's a revolution. India finding its voice, and sending it to the world.

Here's two quick stories from my experience with Nike and Jio.

What I saw with Nike.
They didn't reconnect with people by simply polishing
the message tighter.

Nike has always run on world-class products, marketing
and bold strategy.
The breakthrough came from stripping things back.
From letting real athletes, fans, and trainers take the mic.
Instead of perfect scripts, they put out unpolished videos, raw
training sessions, and stories that looked and felt like life.

That shift wasn't about content alone. It was about trust.
It was about saying,
"We see you, we hear you, and we want to build with you."

Communities don't grow when you talk at them.
They grow when you get involved with them.
Nike rebuilt that bond not through louder campaigns, but through deeper connection, meeting their fans where they lived,
trained, and played.

Jio was the launch of the world's largest tech startup.
In its first year alone, we reached over 100 million customers, people went from almost no digital access, to having information, education, and entertainment at their fingertips.

I worked with the founders and their teams to shape the brand, digital ecosystem, and community from the ground up.
Jio wasn't just a product launch. It was infrastructure, technology, and vision operating at a national scale. But at the center of it all was a simple question.

How do you make digital life feel accessible to over a billion people who had never known it before?

The answer was as radical as it was simple,
give India full access to everything, free, for a limited time.

The impact wasn't just numbers. It was a nation digitally transformed. Families in villages streaming school lessons. Small businesses accessing tools they'd never had before. People from every background suddenly connected, empowered, and able to dream bigger.

That's what makes Jio powerful, it's the heartbeat behind the brand. Not just the technology and products alone, but the human possibility and communities it helped unlock.

The real lesson?

Presence beats polish.
Community building beats single campaigns.
What people remember isn't just the slogan or the logo,
it's the feeling that a brand stood alongside them, not above them,
and helped their passion and community thrive.
And you don't need to work with companies like these, to do this.

I've seen a sneakerhead on Instagram sell hand-painted sneakers by sparking a story of belonging with a simple post, before making a single sale. He understood that community is built through story, experience, enablement and emotion long before it's built through just a product.

The brands that last don't shout.
They hum and flow.
They carry a resonance.
The kind that travels beyond the product itself.
You feel them before you understand them.

If your brand had no ads, campaigns, or logo, would it still be felt?

The next time someone says, "Build a brand,"
maybe start with a breath.
Don't control the brand.
Try to understand it.

If the brand feels alive, are you willing to let it speak for itself?

We worked with an AI and robotics start-up in Silicon Valley. Brilliant engineers. They built a real-world battle-racing car game.

Now we needed to figure out how to launch
both the company and game into the world.

The company invited friends and families some with kids, to test out the game. The moment the AI cars started reading each other, knocking opponents off the track with virtual weapons, the room changed. Every kid wants their toys to come alive.

That thought became the core idea.

We gave each car a personality.

Superpowers.

A backstory.

We presented the company and the game to investors with just two words, that changed everything.

It's Alive.

Takeaways

A brand led by fear will never feel alive.

Connection comes from truth, not polish.

The brands that last stand with people, not above them.
They give real value that fuels passion and community.

Your space to capture the ideas that won't let you go. Write it. Sketch it. Keep it.

Chapter 7
Make New Mistakes.

Originality Lives In Uncertainty.
CREATE: What Can't Be Copied.

Perfection is a trap.
Not because it's unreachable,
but because chasing it keeps you frozen.

I've watched brilliant people stall for years,
waiting for the perfect brief.
The perfect timing.
The perfect team.

It never comes.

Momentum doesn't come from mastery.
It comes from movement.

When I first started, I thought the goal was to get everything right.
Now I know the goal is to get it real. To make better mistakes.
Mistakes that stretch you.
Mistakes that reveal something true.
Mistakes that prove you dared where others wouldn't.

Some of my best work started as a mess.

A wrong tone.
A half-finished thought.
A late-night scribble dropped into a pitch that didn't land
until someone heard the signal buried inside it.

The people who move culture forward?
They're not chasing polish.

They're chasing the spark, at the speed of life.
They trust truth over the comfort of approval.

I once pitched an idea I didn't even put in the presentation,
because everyone said it would fail.
That "failure" sparked a client relationship I still have today.
It transformed that part of the business.

Picture the first messy draft of something iconic.
It didn't look iconic then.

Think of Dyson, sketching and testing 5,126 prototypes
before one actually worked.
Or the artist Basquiat, crossing out words so they
shouted louder in absence.
Or the first ever iPhone keynote presentation,
when Steve Jobs stood on stage with a demo
that was seconds away from breaking.
Or TikTok kids remixing sounds into culture
before music labels even noticed.

None of it was perfect.
But each flaw carried the signal of something new.
Every breakthrough starts messy,
then play turns the mess into momentum.

Play is the ultimate cheat code.
Machines follow scripts. We play and improvise.

Gunpei Yokoi from Nintendo saw someone playing with a broken calculator and turned it into the Game Boy.
Invention through play, technology made human.
Freestyle rap proves the same truth, wordplay in the moment creates sparks no script ever could. Culture alive and unscripted.

Zaha Hadid sketched buildings that looked impossible, her playful design curves broke every architectural rule, and then became landmarks that redefined cities.

Play beats polish every time.

Mistakes aren't a step back.
They're proof you're building in a space no one else has mapped.
Originality doesn't live in your comfort zone.
It lives in the tension of not knowing.

We all say, "fail fast."
But most people still hide when they fall.
They protect themselves.
They repeat what's worked.
They polish the surface instead of upgrading the soul.

The real growth?
It lives in those who own their missteps.

Study them.
Speak to them.
Grow through them.

You don't need to avoid failure.
You need to upgrade the quality of your mistakes.
Mistakes made from courage, not control.
Mistakes that stretch your voice, not shrink it.
Mistakes that reveal extra edges in your work.

This is creative evolution.
This is how your operating system upgrades,
through live testing.
You can't learn by staying invisible.
You learn by trying something that might not land,
and showing up anyway.

Takeaways

Play is the human advantage. The machine can't improvise. We can.

The mistake you're avoiding might be your signature.

The work that lives is never perfect. It's alive.

Wonder

What mistake made you more real, not more careful?
What would you try if you didn't need to get it right,
only to get it true?
What "failure" might actually be your next breakthrough?
What mistake could you make this week that would
scare you into growth?

Practice - Make A Worthy Mistake

Don't aim for perfect. Aim for alive.
Choose one thing you've been putting off, not because it's wrong,
but because it's unfinished, uncertain, or unproven.
Set a twenty-minute timer. Make a version of it.
A draft. A demo. A messy sketch. A voice note.

When the timer ends, don't judge it.
Ask. "What signal showed up in the mess?"

That's where the real work begins.
Better mistakes. Braver work.
That's the upgrade. That's the path to freedom.

Your space to capture the ideas that won't let you go. Write it. Sketch it. Keep it.

Chapter 8
Redesign The Room.

Don't Enter Power. Rebuild It.
CREATE: What Can't Be Copied.

We're taught to chase the room.
The one with the power.
The one where decisions are made.
The one where history gets written.

So we dress the part.
Rehearse the pitch.
Fight for a seat.

Once inside, we realise the table was never built for us.

But what if your role isn't to be included?
What if you're here to rebuild the room entirely?

Stop chasing entry into rooms built to preserve control.
Build your own spaces instead.

Real creators don't just enter systems.
They recode them.
Not out of resentment, but recognition.
The structure itself is outdated.

The rooms that shape today's culture were not built for truth.
They were built to maintain power.
But they're cracking.

What would you build if you stopped asking for entry?

I've done it.
Not by burning everything down,
but by reworking the blueprint.
By inviting in fresh energy.
By letting breath return to spaces too tight to hold anything alive.

I've sat in rooms where fear ran the show.
Where status mattered more than soul.
People too distant to feel the real vibe made the decisions.

Then I built different rooms.
Rooms that felt like oxygen.
Rooms where someone walked in and whispered,
"I didn't know I could exist like this."
Like building a workshop instead of a presentation,
no pitch, no hierarchy, just a circle where every voice mattered
and the problem was solved together.
If a room feels airless, it's not your job to breathe less,
it's to open a window.
Cultural architecture is about designing rooms
that feel like oxygen, not gatekeeping.

Don't mimic the gate. Make a doorway.
Don't seek prestige. Seek resonance.
Don't wait for permission. Design with purpose.

Because the most powerful rooms rarely look impressive,
they feel different.

They carry truth.
They carry tension.
Not the kind that silences, but the kind that awakens.

So if you're building anything real, a studio, a class, a campaign,
a company or a movement, don't just ask who's in the room.

Ask what it was designed to hold,
and whether it can still contain the future you're trying to build.

If the room can't hold your future,
it's time to build a bigger room.

Rebuilding doesn't have to mean risk it all.
You don't need to start with a boardroom or a company.

Start smaller.
Redesign the agenda of a single meeting.
Shift one conversation so truth has space.
Host an online forum where two people feel safe to speak freely.
Create a new process in your team that swaps hierarchy for honesty.
Change one ritual, one table, one rule, and you've already begun.
Big rooms are built out of smaller ones.
This is how you practice without losing your footing.

Takeaways

You don't need entry into their room. Build your own.

Rooms designed for control can't hold the future.

Cultural architecture focuses on creating oxygen, not building gates.

Wonder

What rooms are you still trying to enter, and why?
What structures are you unconsciously repeating,
even as you try to innovate?
What would it mean to build a space that feels like freedom,
not performance?

Practice - Build The Room That Didn't Exist For You

Think of one room you've longed to be in.
Now, instead of chasing entry, design your own version.
Write three qualities that would make it feel alive.
Who's it for?
What's allowed in it?
What's the unspoken rule you'd change?
Then take one small step today, host a conversation,
start a gathering, rewrite a meeting agenda, or launch a private forum.
It doesn't have to be big.
It just has to be true.

You're not here to perform in someone else's room.
You're here to design the one that changes the rules.

Your space to capture the ideas that won't let you go. Write it. Sketch it. Keep it.

Chapter 9
Shape What Only You Can.

Embodied Intelligence In A Machine Age.
CREATE: What Can't Be Copied.

We live in a time of infinite answers and very little understanding.

Ask a machine anything, and it floods you with results.

Strategies. Opinions. Noise.

Data is searchable. Wisdom isn't.

It's your scar tissue, your muscle memory.

But it can't teach you how to read a room.

How to pause instead of perform.

How to feel truth rise in your chest and know, this is the moment.

That kind of knowing can't be copied.

It's not downloaded.

It's lived, earned, embodied.

Some call it wisdom.

Some call it intuition.

I call it creative power.

Because here's the truth. If the machine can make it,
you haven't gone deep enough.

Work with machines, they are great,
and you'll go wider, faster, further.

But only your instinct sets the compass.

Machines multiply possibilities.

You choose the path that means something.

Like in gaming, you don't learn a boss fight by Googling it,
you learn by playing and losing.

The most powerful creators I've met don't have the biggest teams or the loudest voices.

They pay attention.
They know when to press and when to pull back.
When to break the frame, and when to let silence hold the room.
When to put the brush down, not because it's finished,
 but because it's true.

Think of a jazz musician mid-improvisation,
the pause, the off-note, the unexpected riff.
That's what makes the crowd lean in.

Humans are drawn to what feels alive.
Our attention sharpens when something breaks the pattern,
when a gesture or word carries risk, pulse, and presence.
Safe work gets scanned and forgotten.
Brave work transmits.
It doesn't just speak, it reverberates.
It carries a frequency only you could send.
So before you release anything, stop and ask yourself.
Is this just output, or is this me?

We are drowning in data, but starving for the kind of originality that feels inevitable in hindsight.

The work that makes people say,
"Of course it had to be you."

If you vanished tomorrow, what would remain?
The question only you would dare to ask?
The shape only your hand could make?
The scar turned into a symbol, the fracture turned into form?
That's what makes you unforgettable.
Not the trends you chase.
The truth you leave behind.

Your life is the filter. Use it.
Don't just make what's clever.
Make what only your life could have shaped.

The earned wisdom.
The instincts no one trained.
The tenderness discovered in failure, the defiance learned in survival.
Pour that into the work.

Let machines extend the canvas.
Let your humanity decide the stroke.

That's the fingerprint no machine can fake.
That's what people crave.
That's what cuts through the noise.
That's what reminds us we are still human.

Takeaways

Your life is your raw material.
Transform it into a mark no one else could leave.

Embodied scars become originality.

If a machine could make it, it's not yours yet.

Wonder

What has my scar taught me more than any success?
What gesture or riff could only have come from my life?
What story still lives in my body, waiting to be shaped?

Practice - The Fingerprint Test

Choose one piece of work, a draft, a sketch, a half-formed idea.
Circle what feels lived, scarred, embodied.
Now strip away everything else until only that remains.

Ask yourself. Would anyone else in the world have made it this way?
If not, you've found your fingerprint.

Your space to capture the ideas that won't let you go. Write it. Sketch it. Keep it.

Chapter 10
Break The Frame.

Originality Starts Where Obedience Ends.
CREATE: What Can't Be Copied.

The best ideas don't arrive on command.
They slip through the cracks.
They break in when the frame loosens.
When you stop holding the shape together,
something real finds its way through.

Some of the most alive work I've made wasn't in the brief.
It didn't fit the box.
It stretched the edges until the box split open.

Once, in a pitch room, the "safe" idea was already on the table.
Tested. Polished. Guaranteed to land.
But in the corner of a page, I had a raw thought.
Half-formed. A little dangerous.
I showed it anyway.

The room went quiet.
Then someone leaned forward and said,
"That's the one."
Creativity isn't polite.
It doesn't wait for permission.
It doesn't live in categories or comfort.
It wants to be felt.

If it doesn't move you,
why should it move anyone else?

I've seen a child's sketch speak louder than a brand's
ten-week traditional strategy.
I've seen artists walk away from million-dollar deals
just to protect the soul.

Truth has a shape.
And you don't find it by asking what fits.
You find it by breaking what doesn't.

The best creators aren't reckless.
They're disobedient in the right way.
The kind of disobedience that says:
"I heard the brief. Love it.
Now let's take it somewhere unexpected."

Your mind is designed to be surprised.
When something breaks the expected pattern,
your brain fires a prediction error signal.
It lights up, locks in, and remembers.

Expected ideas give the mind nothing to hold onto.
Audacious ideas stick.
They make the brain sit up and pay attention.

The world has plenty of clever ideas.
What we remember are the brave ones.

If no one's a little nervous,
ask yourself if it's really worth making.

Sometimes the soul of the work lives in what you almost killed.
The weird line.
The quiet protest.
The sharp truth you nearly softened.

Not every rebellion survives.
But the ones that do?
They don't just convert.
They cut through.

If you don't feel free making it,
no one will feel free seeing it.

Takeaways

The brain locks onto surprise, rupture is remembered,
polish is forgotten.

Frames hold conformity, breaking them makes space for truth.

Disobedience isn't chaos.
It's clarity where safety has become the default.

Wonder

Where am I still building to fit the frame instead of breaking it?
What idea would make the room nervous, and why am I hiding it?
If safety is the strategy, what signal of truth am I silencing?

Practice - The Rupture Test

Pick one piece of work in progress.
Now break it on purpose.

Remove the neat ending.
Flip the expected order.
Exaggerate the part you almost cut.
Show it raw to a friend, a colleague, or even just yourself out loud.

Watch what happens when the pattern snaps.
That jolt is proof the work is alive.

Your space to capture the ideas that won't let you go. Write it. Sketch it. Keep it.

Part III. LIVE.

Live What Can't Be Faked.

Performance is cheap. Your presence is eternal. To live true in an age of automation is the ultimate awakening. This part is about becoming the signal yourself, so alive, so undeniable, no algorithm can fake it. The real power isn't in competing with machines. It's in showing what only a human can transmit, love, beauty, presence, spirit.

Chapter 11
Art As A Spiritual Weapon.

Beauty Is The Most Radical Force.
LIVE: What Can't Be Faked.

Art isn't decoration, performance or a product for applause.
Art is survival.
It is a heartbeat, an unseen rhythm moving through you,
that no machine can match.
When everything feels stripped away, art is what remains.
When systems collapse, when noise drowns out the signal,
art is water in a desert. The first breath after drowning.
It cuts through.
Your art is a heartbeat born from your scars and your joys.
It beats differently in every body,
but always with the same vital force, it is alive.
Machines can generate images, videos, words, even melodies.
But they cannot suffer. They cannot ache.
They cannot bleed a truth into the world.

A pulse is proof of life. That's what art is.
Proof that you were here.
Proof you felt.
Proof you moved something unseen.
The danger is in forgetting.

We bury art under traditional strategy, speed, spectacle.
We reduce it to a campaign, a KPI, a line item in a presentation.
But the real work of art isn't in how many see it.
It's in how deeply it shifts the ones who do.

A true work of art rewires your whole resonance.
It shifts how you create, how you speak, how you show up.
It is not software. It is soul.
And a heartbeat cannot be scaled.
Its power is in how it's felt, not how it's measured.
So make beauty unavoidable.
Not because it sells, but because it saves.
Because when the lights cut out and the charts are gone, the only thing left will be the beat of what you made.

Your art is your pulse in the world.
Guard it.
Feed it.
Release it.
Because no machine can carry your energy into tomorrow,
only you can.

Takeaways

Beauty isn't decoration. It's the signal of possibility and belonging, like light cutting through the dark.

The right piece of art doesn't just catch the eye,
it changes the body and the air in the room.

Art is a heartbeat no machine can mimic,
a beat of truth carried by love and defiance.

Wonder

What's the heartbeat you've created that no one clapped for?
What if art isn't decoration at all, but the pulse that keeps us going?
How might my work be not an escape, but a way for someone
else to survive?

Your space to capture the ideas that won't let you go. Write it. Sketch it. Keep it.

Chapter 12
Own Happy.

Redefining Success On Your Terms.
LIVE: What Can't Be Faked.

Success used to mean the skyline.
The office. The title. The meetings.
The endless climb that made me feel like I mattered.
I chased recognition like it was oxygen.
I got it.
And still felt hollow.
That's the part no one tells you.
You can win the game and lose yourself.
You can tick every box and still feel something essential is missing.

I've met people with the "dream life" who looked empty.
And others quiet, honest, awake who felt so alive their presence made the noise seem laughable.
That's when I started asking a better question.
What does happiness actually look like for me?

Not the industry's version.
Not social media's highlight reel.
Not the legacy someone else decided I should want.
Mine.

Happiness isn't a finish line.
It's a window you open every morning,
even if the view outside hasn't changed.

It's the signal you feel before the world tells you what to want.

Here's what I found.

Happiness is the hum in the air before the day begins.
Steam rising from a cup in your hands.
Uncontrollable laughter at work that catches you midweek, mid-mess.
The sea's energy colliding with the shore.
It's building something amazing, with people who believe and feel it.
A late-night idea that could change everything for the better.
A meeting where possibility lands in someone's eyes.

It's good food, good conversation, with good people.
A walk with a friend who reminds you who you are.
It's the quiet knowledge you're shaping something
worth leaving behind.
Creating without chasing.
Sleeping deeply.
Leading from alignment, not exhaustion.
That's my kind of happiness.

Owning your happiness is the most radical form of freedom.

Because everything around you is designed to sell
someone else's version of success.
More. Faster. Louder.
But real power is quieter.
It's designing a life you don't need to escape from.
Here's the truth about happiness.
Your mind can't sustain a constant high.
It isn't wired for endless hustle.

It craves moments of safety, connection, and meaning.
When you give it those, your nervous system settles.
Your focus sharpens.
You feel at home in your own life.
That's why owning happiness isn't about a peak moment.
But more about making enough space for grounded moments
to keep returning.

I think of a founder I know.
He turned down a high-paying role that would've doubled their status
overnight, because it meant less time with his kids.
He chose Saturday mornings in the park
over applause in a bigger boardroom.
From the outside, it looked like a step back.
But every time I saw him after, he looked freer. Lighter. More himself.
That's the kind of wealth you can't measure, but you can feel.

It won't always look impressive.
It might disappoint others.
It might cost you rooms, titles, clients.

But what do you gain?
Peace.
Clarity.
Self-respect.
The freedom to live on your own terms.

That's what happiness feels like.
Not the smile-for-the-camera version.
The kind that heals everything.
And once it's yours, no one can take it away.

Takeaways

Happiness is more than a peak, it's a rhythm you design.

Your nervous system thrives on safety, connection, and meaning, not more drama and hustle.

Real success is a life you don't need to escape from.

Wonder

What does happiness feel like in my body, not in someone else's feed?
Where have I been performing success instead of feeling it?
What would change if joy, not goals, set the direction?

Practice - The Happiness Audit

For one week, write down one moment each day that felt alive and happy. Not impressive. Not productive. Just true.

At the end of the week, circle the patterns.
Those are your real metrics.
Now ask. What would shift if I built more of my life around these?

Your space to capture the ideas that won't let you go. Write it. Sketch it. Keep it.

Chapter 13
There Are No Answers.

Presence In The Unknown.
LIVE: What Can't Be Faked.

I used to think everyone wanted certainty.
A path.
A method.
A promise that if you followed the right steps,
you'd land somewhere good.

It's how we're taught to live.
There's a right way, a proven system,
a formula for everything, even for life.
What I learned is this,
the people willing to walk without a map
often create the real path.
For me, creativity rarely lives in clarity.
It doesn't live in the formula.
It doesn't live in the plan.
It lives in the mist.

I once left a secure role in a great company for a secret,
unknown project.
I didn't know where it would lead.
The mist didn't clear, but I walked anyway.

It felt like a blank screen, awkward,
but that's where everything begins.

I still remember the first night.

A bare room, mismatched chairs, and a single whiteboard already covered in half-erased sketches. The air smelled like burnt coffee and nervous energy. There were no glossy presentations, no safety nets, just a handful of us staring at an idea that barely made sense on paper.

I can still hear the hum of the AC, the way one person drummed their fingers on the table while another scribbled numbers that didn't add up yet.

And then, almost to the room itself,
someone said quietly, "This could transform everything."
It wasn't certainty. It wasn't proof.
It was a door cracked open in the mist,
and the decision to walk through.

That project became the launch of one of the world's largest tech startups.
A movement that changed a nation for the better.
The unknown doesn't always hand you clarity.
Sometimes it hands you texture, weight,
and a kind of quiet you can trust.

The people I've seen shift culture aren't the ones
with the cleanest answers.
They're the ones who can stand inside ambiguity without flinching.
Who resist the urge to control.
Who stay honest when it's messy.
Who keep moving even when the ground isn't stable yet.

It might look like chaos from the outside.
But to me, it's courage.
It's intelligence.
It's presence.

The thing about uncertainty is the brain doesn't like it.
When the outcome is unclear, it searches for patterns
to predict the future.
That's why so many rush to fill the unknown with something,
or anything that feels solid, even if it's wrong.

Your brain craves certainty,
but creativity requires you to resist that pull,
to trust the unknown instead of rushing to fill it.
That's because when you step into uncertainty,
your brain is forced to light up in new ways.

It starts scanning for connections, noticing patterns,
and building fresh pathways.
I've learned that if you can hold your ground when the map is blank,
you train yourself to notice more.

To connect dots others can't see.
To build not from panic, but from possibility.
I used to think leadership meant having it all figured out.
Now I know better.
It means knowing what matters when everything else feels like noise.
It means staying calm in the uncertainty.
It means not copying what worked for someone else.

It means choosing truth over technique.
It means using every new tool to make something more human, not less.

Not knowing isn't a weakness.
But the beginning of real creativity.

If you feel lost right now, it might mean you're not pretending.
It might mean you're exactly where you need to be.

The only thing worse than being lost is pretending you're not.

Hold the unknown with reverence.
Sit with it.
Let the mist teach you what second-hand facts can't.

This OS you're building doesn't run on shortcuts.
It runs on soul.

The soul that builds something honest, even if it's slow.
Even if it's uncertain.
Even if it goes against what you've been taught.
The path ahead won't be written by maps, it will be written by you.

Takeaways

Uncertainty isn't the enemy, it's the raw material of creativity.

Most rush to escape the unknown, but staying in it gives you an edge.

Presence in the mist builds trust, clarity,
and the ability to create what's never been done.

Wonder

Where am I forcing answers I don't need yet?
What part of me is trying to skip the uncertainty instead
of learning from it?
What would I build if I trusted the not-knowing?

Your space to capture the ideas that won't let you go. Write it. Sketch it. Keep it.

Chapter 14
The Creative Spirit.

Who You Are, Is What You Make.
LIVE: What Can't Be Faked.

Some things vanish the moment they're seen.
Others echo for years.

The difference?
Not budget.
Not reach.
Not even talent.

It's spirit.
Aliveness is the flex. Not the highlight reel,
the actual current running through you.
Think Bob Marley or Frank Ocean, music that feels like life itself,
not performance.
Not a mood.
Not a playlist.
Not a voice you switch on in a pitch.

Spirit is the human pulse that cannot be faked.
It is the part of you only you can bring.
I've watched people chase tools, templates, platforms,
but none of it matters if the work isn't alive and kicking.

You can feel it when someone shows up.
Not to impress, but to express.
Not to dominate, but to witness.
To translate something only they could feel.

When I encounter work that moves me,
I don't ask, How did they do this?
I ask, Who were they when they made it?
That's what cuts through.
Not polish, but pulse.

The real creative work is who you become along the way.
The one who stops performing.
The one who feels everything, then finds the words.
The one who hits send with a racing heart.

We're wired to detect the real thing.
The micro-pause in a voice.
The imperfection in a brushstroke.
The shadow in a picture that wasn't posed.
The shift in pacing when someone cares more than they planned to.
We don't always know why something feels alive,
but our bodies recognise it instantly. And remember.
When we over-optimise,
when we trade emotion for efficiency,
when we build the algorithm and forget the pulse,
creativity becomes content.
Wonder becomes marketing.

Don't lose the spirit behind the spark.

Creativity defies formulas.
It lives in freedom, in tension.

In the quiet.
In the risk of saying something honest.

Raw enough to cut through.
True enough to stay.
That's what makes someone pause,
not to consume, but to remember.

Takeaways

Spirit is the invisible force that makes work linger long after it's seen.

People instinctively recognise and remember what feels alive.

Efficiency without emotion kills the pulse
that makes creativity matter.

Wonder

When was the last time I made something that scared me,
in a good way?
Where have I traded spirit for a comfortable way of doing things?
What would I create if I trusted that the most important
thing I offer is me?

Your work will age.
Trends will fade.
But if you put your presence in it, it will live on.

Your space to capture the ideas that won't let you go. Write it. Sketch it. Keep it.

Chapter 15
Love Over Everything.

The Legacy That Outlasts All.
LIVE: What Can't Be Faked.

After the pitches.
After the pressure.
After the launch, the feedback, the metrics, the applause.

What remains?

Not the slides.
Not the sound bite.
Not the status updates.

What's left is love.

The love you carried into the room.
The love you wove into the work.
The glance across the table that said, without words, I'm with you,
when no one clapped,
when no one said thank you.

Love holds what no one else sees,
the tension, the weight, the entire room.

It's what makes a project feel true.
A team feel safe.
A stranger feel seen.

Even so, we rarely name it.
In the boardroom, love gets buried beneath the numbers.
It doesn't glow on a chart.
It doesn't scale.

Yet after the noise dies down, it's the only thing that stays.

I've been in rooms starved of love,
where everything felt tight, cold, and quietly breaking.

I've worked in rooms where love was present,
and something opened,
not just between people, but inside the work itself.
The thing about human beings is,
we are shaped by the emotional climate we move through.
When love is present, our guard drops.

Our creativity expands.
We take bolder risks.
We see possibility instead of limits.
Love doesn't make things soft.
It makes them undeniable.

Love shows up as truth-telling, even when it's uncomfortable.
It shows up in listening without needing to win.
It shows up in building things that leave people better
than you found them.
It shows up in paying attention, even when there's nothing to gain.

Love is not weakness.
It's the most disruptive force on Earth.

It cuts through noise.
It repairs what performance broke.
It transcends scale.
It sustains what hype can't.

When people feel loved, they speak up.
They soften.
They stay.
So as you move through this new OS, ask yourself.
Am I creating from fear or from love?
Am I leading with control or with trust?
Am I building for applause or for impact?

Love is the whole point.
Everything else is just a backdrop.
In the end, what remains is the love you carry,
and how it shaped the lives and spaces you touch.

Takeaways

Love is the most enduring currency you can invest in your work and leadership.

An emotional climate sparks creativity, strategy helps channel it.

Fear shuts the door. Love throws it wide open.

Wonder

Where in my work has love been present, but unnamed?
What would happen if I let love lead, not just in life, but in creation?
What if love isn't the soft ending, but the strongest beginning?

Let that be the code beneath it all.
Love over everything, because freedom without love
is just running away. Always.

Practice - A Human Vow

Write a vow to what makes you human, your craft,
your people, your truth.
Keep it short enough to say in one breath.
Speak it aloud today.
Notice how it changes the room, even if you're the only one in it.

Your space to capture the ideas that won't let you go. Write it. Sketch it. Keep it.

Part IV. INTEGRATE.

Live What You Teach. Create What You Live.

Knowledge without action fades. Creativity without grounding floats away. Presence without purpose burns out. Integration is where it all fuses, where your wisdom shapes your work, your work reflects your life, and your life carries a signal no machine can imitate. This part is about alignment, about living so whole that nothing is wasted, every scar, every insight, every spark becomes part of the operating system only you can run.

Chapter 16
The Operating System In Motion.

How To Live It, Share It, And Scale It Without Selling Your Soul.
INTEGRATE: Live What You Teach. Create What You Live.

Some things aren't meant to be finished.
They're meant to be carried.
Lived.
Built into the way you move.

This can never be something you install once and walk away from.
It's how you breathe.
How you show up.

It begins where performance ends.
So let truth lead now.

Teach, not from theory, but from what the pain taught you.
Create, not to be heard, but to say something real and memorable.
Live, not for applause, but because it feels true in your soul.

This chapter won't wrap things up.
It's a mirror.
For who you are when no one's watching.
How you move when validation stops.

We are wired to seek alignment.
When your actions match your values, the mind settles,
the body trusts, and others feel it too.
When they don't, the dissonance leaks through
no matter how polished the performance.

Courage is integration. It's the moment you stop scrolling and actually act. It's when alignment stops being theory and becomes a step, a word, a decision.
Harmony is found in the smallest moments.
When you stop chasing approval and let what's real guide your steps.

Start here.

Teach. What can't be Googled.
Wisdom over information.
You can store facts anywhere.
The truths only you can pass on are rare.
Share the ones earned the hard way, the ones that live in your bones.
Teach from there.
That's where the real power is.

Create. What can't be copied.
Soul over output.
Tools can multiply what you make.
But only you can make something alive.
Make what carries your edge, your freedom.
Protect it.
That's what makes it unforgettable.

Live. What can't be faked.
Presence over performance.
Life will keep moving faster,
the real rebellion is to stay fully here.
Not the polished version,
but the real you.
The one people feel in the room before you speak.

Courage isn't abstract.
It's saying no to the toxic collaboration everyone else is
too afraid to call out.
It's walking away from the safe job when your soul knows it's over.
It's the choice that costs you something, and frees you anyway.

Keep living it.
That's the method.
That's the proof.
When it feels like nothing's happening,
something is.
By living it, you're changing the energy.
You're not just building something.
You're becoming the power behind it.

Takeaways

When your actions match your values, people feel it immediately.

Harmony means stripping away what's false.

When you stop performing, you start transmitting.

Wonder

Where am I still shape-shifting to be accepted?
What part of my truth is ready to come out of hiding?
How would I move if I trusted I'm already enough?

You don't need a louder voice.
You need a cleaner truth.

Practice - Move As One

Let your life become the proof of what you believe.
Pick one space in your life where you've been performing.
Pause.
What does wholeness look like there?
Not perfection just presence without performance.
Choose one small act this week that expresses the truth without apology. Not louder. Just clearer.

When your voice and your values move together, that's integration.

Your space to capture the ideas that won't let you go. Write it. Sketch it. Keep it.

Chapter 17
Live Transmission.

The Future Won't Be Built. It'll Be Felt.
INTEGRATE: Live What You Teach. Create What You Live.

The future won't ask for perfection.
It will ask for energy.
Not clarity, but charge.
Not credentials, but connection.

Those with the most answers won't lead the next era.
It'll be shaped by those who feel deeply,
and share what matters in the moments,
the unscripted,
the unfinished,
the unmistakably human.
You're not here to outpace machines.
You're here to out-feel them.

The system has shifted.
We don't just build with bricks now.
We build with emotion.
We build with truth.
When you're focused,
your voice becomes a vibrant wave that cuts through anything,
shaped by the truth you've lived.

The machines don't know what to do with that.
It can't code intuition.
It can't fake the truth.
It can't feel your fire.
Only you can.

People move toward what feels alive.
It's how we're wired.

We lean into resonance that carry warmth, tension, and truth,
because somewhere deep inside, we know that's where
possibility lives.

It's not persuasion.
It's recognition.
The moment someone feels you're real,
they stop scanning and start listening.

So what now?
Now you lead, not from polish, but from passion.
Now you stop rehearsing, and start radiating.
Now, you become the message.
Your studio.
Your company.
Your classroom.
Your kitchen.
That next sketch, that quiet idea, that one conversation,
they're not just outputs. They're openings.

If you show up fully, without shrinking,
you don't just change the moment.
You shift the direction of what's coming.

Don't chase the future.
Tune into it.
You are the current.
You are the transmission.
You are the system, alive and moving.

You're not here to ride the next wave.
You're here to become it, to move with a freedom nothing can contain.

So tune in.
Turn it on.
Send it out.

Takeaways

Energy outlasts perfection.

People follow what feels alive, not what's most polished.

Your presence is felt before it's heard.

Protect it. Amplify it. Send it out.

Wonder

Where in my life have I been holding back,
showing up as less than I am?
What would change if I let truth set the pace, not pressure?
Where is my energy already alive, just waiting for me to trust it?

Your space to capture the ideas that won't let you go. Write it. Sketch it. Keep it.

Outro.

If you've made it this far, congratulations.
That's already a win.

By now, you've carried these stories, questions, and codes through your own filter. Something in you has already shifted.
Not louder. Just truer.
Some days you'll lose the signal.
Other days, it will catch you off guard,
like a song you forgot you loved.
When that happens, stay honest. Stay awake.

This was never a book to finish.
It's a rhythm you return to.
A way of moving that starts deep in your core and works its way out into everything you touch.
Lead with your light.
Paint with your scars.
Create from the fire that only burns in you.

This is your Freedom Operating System.
Your code for freedom in a new era.
Teach what can't be Googled.
Create what can't be copied.
Live what can't be faked.

When the choice comes, because it always does.
Choose freedom over performance every time.
Because in the end, it's not about keeping up.
It's about keeping you.

Above all.
Live the life only you were created to live.

You are the method now.
Live it. Feel it. Be free.
Make the life you want to live and leave something timeless behind.
Go live.

Peace
Mehta

www.ingramcontent.com/pod-product-compliance
Lightning Source LLC
Chambersburg PA
CBHW071211070526
44584CB00019B/2998